STEPHEN DREDGE

First Time Home Buyer: How to Buy a Home in Utah 101

Tips and Tricks for Purchasing your First Home; What every first time homebuyer should know.

Copyright © 2024 by Stephen Dredge

All rights reserved. No part of this publication may be reproduced, stored or transmitted in any form or by any means, electronic, mechanical, photocopying, recording, scanning, or otherwise without written permission from the publisher. It is illegal to copy this book, post it to a website, or distribute it by any other means without permission.

Stephen Dredge asserts the moral right to be identified as the author of this work.

Stephen Dredge has no responsibility for the persistence or accuracy of URLs for external or third-party Internet Websites referred to in this publication and does not guarantee that any content on such Websites is, or will remain, accurate or appropriate.

Designations used by companies to distinguish their products are often claimed as trademarks. All brand names and product names used in this book and on its cover are trade names, service marks, trademarks and registered trademarks of their respective owners. The publishers and the book are not associated with any product or vendor mentioned in this book. None of the companies referenced within the book have endorsed the book.

All information contained within this book is from first hand experience and years of working in the industry. There are no references as I am citing my own knowledge rather than online sources. However if you research any of the topics you will find that they are all accurate.

First edition

This book was professionally typeset on Reedsy.
Find out more at reedsy.com

> "Buy land, they're not making it anymore."
>
> — MARK TWAIN

Contents

Preface	ii
1 Understanding WHY you want to buy a home	1
2 Apply for a loan (Prequalification)	14
3 Create a Must Have and a Nice to Have list	22
4 Start Seeing Homes!	26
5 Writing The Offer	29
6 Under Contract	34
7 The Closing and Post Settlement	40
8 Summary	45
9 Bonus Chapter: ROI and Investment Basics	47
Testimonials	53
About the Author	58

Preface

Here are a couple quick thoughts to set the stage

1. The purpose of this book is to provide you with a basic working knowledge of what to expect when buying a home, especially if this is your first time. The tip of the iceberg, so to speak. This book is NOT intended to make you a real estate expert. For that you are going to have to take hundreds of hours of classes, pass exams, and practice real estate for years. After you're finished reading you WILL have a good idea of how the process works and what to expect as you pass certain milestones in the buying process.
2. People need 3 basic things to survive: food, water and shelter. You're here reading because you recognize the importance of OWNING your own shelter (home). It's a basic survival instinct that can be traced back to the dawn of time. Since the days of cavemen, locations that provided shelter from the elements and protection from the wild have been sought after. As you read the following pages you'll learn about digging deep into your core for the reasons WHY you're buying a home. You'll learn about the mechanics of such a large purchase and what to do once the papers are signed. Then, before you know it, you're excitedly eating a pizza getting ready to sleep on an air mattress on your first night in the new home!

WHO IS INVOLVED

There are 7 main entities/businesses involved in a transaction for a buyer. I will reference all throughout the book.

1. **Your Realtor/Brokerage**: The middle man or woman. Main point of contact for questions and concerns. Ensures that all entities on the buyers side AND sellers side are working in unison. Negotiates on behalf of you, the clients.
2. **Your Lender/bank:** In charge of the money and making sure that you, the buyer can be ready financially to purchase a home. They will need a lot of information from you.
3. **Your Title company**: Collects documents from both sides (buyer and seller) to make sure that everything matches up. Does background checks on the property so there are no liens or lawsuits involving the home. Provides chain of title and title insurance. Collects and disburses funds at settlement.
4. **The seller's Realtor or Brokerage** - Same function as your realtor except you will not have any contact with them.
5. **The seller's title company** - Same function as your title company except you will likewise not have any contact with them.
6. **The Buyer** - You
7. **The Seller** - The owners of the subject property

So without further adieu, let's jump into it!

1

Understanding WHY you want to buy a home

Before we get into the mechanics of buying a home. We need to first, better understand WHY you are even thinking about making this large purchase and how to navigate the emotions involved. Believe it or not, this is the first step to buying.

CHALLENGE - you'll want to do this, trust me

I highly recommend you STOP, take a few moments, and really think about **WHY** you want to buy a home. Grab some paper or your phone and write those reasons down. Then ask yourself, why those? Write down the deeper meanings behind the reasons (the reason for the reason). You can go as deep as you wish until you feel that you're satisfied with your answer. Then come back and finish reading this chapter. Once you're finished with the chapter, go back to your list of reasons and add to them, dig even deeper to really get to the root of the reason. (This will come in handy later)

YOUR WHY - What will buying/building a home do for you?

Every person comes to a point in their life when they ask themselves one or more of the following questions:

- "Should I buy a house?"
- "Do I want to keep renting and paying off someone else's mortgage?"
- "Should I move out of my parents basement?"
- "What are the benefits to owning a home vs renting?"
- "Can I even afford to buy one?"
- "Is it worth it?"
- "All the rich people in the world have real estate, maybe I should too."

Chances are you have had some of these same thoughts and that's why you are reading this book. Or we've been talking and I gave you a copy! One of the largest growth points in our individual progression (or joint progression if you are married) is to take the giant leap of faith and become a homeowner! Don't get me wrong, It's not a requirement or a necessity; but over the course of the last couple thousand years (and probably since the dinosaurs went extinct), moving out and securing a place of your own has been a pivotal part of life!

There is something empowering and liberating about OWNING your own piece of land, something that you can call YOURS. A place where your kids can come home after a rough day at school and feel safe, warm and welcomed; and maybe even make a snowman in the wintertime. Maybe it's the first step in your investment/retirement scheme and you

UNDERSTANDING WHY YOU WANT TO BUY A HOME

can just picture yourself using this home to purchase several others a few years down the road! Or perhaps it's a place where you can invite your friends or family over for a BBQ or movie night and say, "come over to MY house." Somewhere that you can decorate for Christmas, Honnaka, the 4th of July, Halloween or whenever you want for as long as you want. Maybe you need to have a place to play catch with your dog outside and cuddle up with her in bed at night. The point is, we, for the most part, as humans, crave those feelings of liberty and being in control of our lives. And when you own something, you can make it yours and do whatever you want, law-permitting of course!

In my experience I have seen potential homeowners' "reasons" trump any price tag, monthly payment or road block. If your goals, ambitions and dreams are powerful enough then you CAN and WILL be able to make them a reality and have everything you've dreamt about. Full Transparency, when you start to buy a home, you will most likely be flooded with lots of emotions and doubts.

> What is it they say about dreams? 'If your dreams don't scare you, they are not big enough!'

Story Time

Take for example the story of Bill and Joanne (With their permission I will tell you a brief part of their story. Their real names have been excluded in order to maintain anonymity).

Prior to the present day, they were living in a slightly rougher part of town due to their financial situation, or so they thought.

They had always told themselves that they would move as soon as things got better or they felt more comfortable with home prices and interest rates, or when she graduated from school. Before they knew it 3 years had passed Joanne had graduated and birthed a child. Having a baby really started to change their perspective causing them to be much more focused on moving to a place they felt more comfortable raising a child. But the task just seemed incredibly daunting and expensive.

One night at about 3 am there was an incessant pounding at their front door. Bill was fast asleep but Joanne jolted awake and began to shake Bill's arm. "Do you hear that?" she said with a hint of panic in her voice. After Bill had woken they listened for a few moments and the pounding continued. Bill nervously peeked through the bedroom curtain to try and catch a glimpse and could see, from the side, that there was indeed someone at the door. A man, shirtless, swaying back and forth pounding his fist on the door while rattling the locked door handle trying to force it open.

Bill's instincts immediately kicked into overdrive as he thought of protecting his wife and newborn child in the adjacent room. He knew that he was going to be the first line of defense should anything happen. He swiftly, and quietly retrieved the pistol from the safe next to the bed, chambered a round and proceeded to the front door. Joanne had 911 dialed and ready to call.

Bill nervously yelled through the door "Who is it?!" No answer. He yelled again, silence. He shakily brought the pistol to bear and peered through the front of the door widow while simultaneously flipping the front porch light on. As he parted the blinds of the front door window and looked through the glass he could see that not only was the man shirtless but that he had blood running down his face. At the same instant the man on the other side began to pound even harder at a much faster rate all while trying to work the handle of the locked door.

As Bill was about to yell at the intruder to "get the heck off his property or he would call the cops, and that he had a gun and was not afraid to use it to protect his wife and child," a vehicle sped up and screeched to a halt. The individual in the passenger seat yelled something inaudible toward the house. The man at the front door stumbled back and began to proceed toward the vehicle. Bill opened the door. The passenger yelled at the man to "Get in the car! What are you doing!" Then she yelled toward Bill apologizing for the mix up and explained that the man was drunk and forgot where he lived.

Shocked, with his blood pumped full of adrenaline and heart pounding out of his chest, Bill managed to get out "that's alright." The car sped away and all was quiet again. It took a while for the adrenaline to wear off, but even then Bill and Joanne barely slept a wink until the sun came up.

All of the excuses and "reasons" they had for not moving were immediately thrown out the window and they set out to find a place they could call their own. A few months later they found a property, purchased it and moved. Now, because of their leap of faith into the unknown Bill and Joanne are in an incredible neighborhood surrounded by great people! Not to mention the amount of equity they have already built up in their property! It was a win win! They were able to achieve their goal of moving to a place they felt was right to raise their family AND they now have a significant amount of equity in their home.

I know this might be a slightly more extreme example than you were expecting, but it illustrates the point well. DO NOT let the logistics get in the way of your goals, dreams and desires; which in this case was the safety of Bill and Joanne's family. If you let all the reasons not to buy a home get the best of you, you'll end up 30 years from now still renting from someone else who was able to push past their fears and make it happen. If you want it bad enough, nothing can stop you. Sure it may take planning, paying off some debts, getting a different job, readjusting expectations etc, but it can be done... if you want it!

Find your WHY's, write them down somewhere you can see them everyday. Make a vision board, record yourself saying them and play it every morning. I don't care what it is, but do something so you can see your reasons why every day. This, in turn, will keep you grounded and help you work through any obstacles that may arise.

This method can work equally as well for anything you want in life. Maybe there is a car you really want, a trip you want to go on, a promotion, that new phone etc. Write down the goal, and the WHY you want it (what it will do for you) somewhere you can see it EVERY DAY. You'd be surprised to look back on that vision board a few years later and see just how well you did!

THE EMOTIONS - Buying a home can feel simultaneously uncomfortable and incredible

Psst... I'll let you in on a little secret that no other Realtor will tell you. The process of buying a home will likely cause you to experience many, if not all, of the emotions on the emotional spectrum. It's just the natural human response to what happens when we START to do hard things! Think about how we are wired down to the very core. We feel uncomfortable, nervous, scared, excited, enthusiastic etc when we experience something completely new or foreign.

Think of a high school teenager getting ready to ask his crush to the dance. You can bet that as he gets ready to head over to her house or approach her at school to ask, that he's having second thoughts, his palms are sweating and his voice begins to crack from the pressure. Or maybe an aspiring leader at work is asked to give her first presentation to the CEO and board members for the next product launch. You can imagine her hands shaking slightly, maybe her mind goes blank for a few seconds and she tries to regain her composure and begins the presentation with all eyes on her.

Both of these examples illustrate feelings that we experience right before, or during, us doing something uncomfortable or new. I'm sure you've had plenty of instances where you knew you needed to do something but the waves of doubt, nervousness, uncertainty and voices of others started to creep back in; screaming at you to put yourself into a more comfortable situation. By pushing through our doubts and fears we will be able to "go to the dance with the person we want" or "make it onto the boss's radar for that next big promotion."

FIRST TIME HOME BUYER: HOW TO BUY A HOME IN UTAH 101

If buying a home were easy peasy then EVERYONE WOULD DO IT. And I have news for you, if it's your first home or your 50th home, chances are you will experience a myriad of emotions and have to work through those mentally. You will get better at curbing those emotions over time as you become more experienced, but they will always be there. It's what makes us human. And, if you've hired a realtor, such as myself, then they will be able to help you navigate the seemingly complex highway of emotions grounding you back to your WHY.

If you know what to look for you can better prepare yourself. Throughout the buying process you will most likely have some of the following thoughts or concerns:

- We have been going through our finances and it just really doesn't look like we can afford it anymore. (after you have already been prequalified by a lender/bank).
- Someone told me to wait until rates or prices came down.
- I need to save 20% in order to buy a home.
- I think maybe I should just wait until I get my next promotion at work.
- My aunt/uncle/grandfather/friend/coworker said I shouldn't and that I am insane for buying a home.
- Some good deals on flights just came up to Europe for the trip we've always wanted.
- Am I really going to do this? This is something only old people do.
- I just dont think it's worth it anymore.
- Maybe it would be best after the baby came.
- We'll start looking again after summer is over, it's just too busy for us right now.
- I've been talking with a friend that said they might sell their house

UNDERSTANDING WHY YOU WANT TO BUY A HOME

to us for a good deal, let's wait and see what happens.

Now don't get me wrong, there is a chance that some of these concerns or speed bumps are very valid and need to be addressed; but in my experience, the vast majority of the time it is simply your brain trying to give you reasons to pull the plug. It's your fight or flight mode kicking in. Your brain tells you that this is going to be uncomfortable because you've never done it before. It is the "unknown" the "wildcard." And when you have those doubts or when others tell you you're crazy; it's then that you need to pull out your list of REASONS WHY and remind yourself why this is so important to you.

Let me reiterate, if you want it bad enough, then go and get it.

Side bar: The Federal housing price index for quarter 4 of 2023 states that since 1991 Utah's house pricing index has INCREASED by 596.1%. This is the HIGHEST percentage of every other state; with Montana and Colorado at a 594.39% and 590.76% increase respectively. Compare this to the national average of 311.88% and I'd say that with a track record like that, real estate in Utah is a safe place to put your hard earned dollars. (You can find all this on FHFA.gov)

And if it is not important to you to buy a house then THAT IS OK, it's not for everyone. I'm not going to sugarcoat it. Sometimes people just hate the idea of owning a home or legitimately can't afford it and are not willing to make plans to improve their situation to make it happen in the future; or they let their fears of not being able to control the uncontrollable dictate their actions. But that's not you, otherwise you wouldn't be reading this book. You KNOW what you want and are ready to get out there and make it happen.

One of the most common reasons I hear for not buying a home is "the market is going to crash! I'm just going to wait for that to happen and then buy my home for pennies on the dollar." I Hate to break it to you, but that isn't going to happen. If you're really curious then come talk to me and we can talk shop, go over the economics, trends and safeguards that have been put into place to ensure that won't happen.

BUUUUT Let's pretend for a second that it did happen; if the market crashes and the world goes down the crapper then it won't matter how much money you've "saved" by renting, and you'll have a lot more doubts about whats going to happen next. What will matter will be how prepared you are, how many guns and ammo you have and if you have a place to go! And if the market does crash but the world doesn't go down the drain, then big corporations, businesses, and private investors will be in a line a mile long itching to buy up all of the cheap/foreclosed real estate. The person not getting any piece of the pie will be the overly cautious guy who's been waiting to buy for 25 years. He's going to be outbid and muscled out every time until he settles on something much less than he wanted.

The reality is that people need only a few basic things to survive, food, water and shelter. Shelter - or real estate - is a finite resource, meaning that there is not an infinite amount of it out there. And as more and more of it is purchased, less and less of it is available; which in turn, increases the price tag. And here in Utah there is a limited amount of space that can even be built on.

When you take into account the vast amounts of protected land that is mandated for wildlife protection, BLM land, forest service land etc. then it narrows the amount of buildable land even further. And with the ever growing population of utah, so grows the demand for housing options. Simple supply and demand. If there is a demand out there (which there most certainly is) then people will continue to buy. But I digress.

OUTSIDE INFLUENCES - You're going to want to read this section!

Remember earlier on in this chapter where we talked about all doubts and reasons your brain will come up with to not move forward with buying a home? Well it does not stop there. In my experience almost EVERY single first time homebuyer has a family member, friend, colleague etc that they would trust with their life. Chances are you have one or more of these types of people in your life as well.

Seeking secondary advice is something I highly recommend. Heck, I do it on the daily! My dad is a huge help to me in any decision making process. However, when it comes to purchasing a house I would caution you on how much weight you give outside opinions. Any opinion from a trusted source is valid and needs to be taken into consideration. But what also needs to be taken into consideration is the relevance of the opinion. Is it outdated, heavily biased, based on a certain time, not current with what's happening in the market, or skewed by 1 bad experience?

For example: If you go and ask your grandparents for advice on buying a home or tell them you are thinking about buying one, they may respond with something like "It's impossible for you," or "We bought our first house for $46,000 and 12 raspberries." or "rates are too high, just wait for the market to crash."

Or if you have a relative that was a real estate agent for 20 years but has not been actively working in the real estate space for a while, they might caution you to beware and that it's a terrible time to buy.

Please do not misunderstand what I am saying; good advice from a trusted individual is always good to have. You're smart and I know that you'll be able to pick out which advice to take to heart and which advice to leave behind. Being misled by trusted individuals with good intentions and incorrect information is a very real thing. I see it happen every day.

And then before you know it, it's 5-10 years down the road and you recognize that if you would have overcome those fears and purchased a home back then, that you would have "X" amount of equity, a place for your kids to run around, not be renting, and on track to make your dreams a reality. Because, to be perfectly transparent, if you are not heavily involved in any particular industry, then your opinion of that industry is usually very far from being correct. And your sources stem from either the mainstream media or a singular experience you had at some point in your life.

So before you blindly follow a trusted source or sources, ask yourself the following questions:

- Is this person up to date with the current real estate market (20+ hours per week)?
- Has this person purchased or sold a home in the last 30 days?
- Does this person have an education that revolves around real estate, investing, lending?
- Does this person receive their information from anywhere besides the news?

UNDERSTANDING WHY YOU WANT TO BUY A HOME

If you answered "no" to ANY of those questions then all of their advice and what they tell you to do should be filtered and double checked with a professional.

2

Apply for a loan (Prequalification)

Now that we know why you need to purchase a home and that you are ready and able to fly over every mental speed bump that gets put in your path, let's dig into how it actually works and the mechanics involved: It's time to get prequalified with a lender or a bank. Let me preface by saying that I am not a Lender and that you should reach out to a lender or bank for any specific questions. The following information is what I have picked up over my years as a Realtor.

BASIC TERMINOLOGY

- **Lender**: Dedicated loan officer working for a company dedicated to helping people with loans for homes, businesses etc. These guys may have access to more expansive loan programs and options and subsequently may be more experienced.
- **Bank:** Traditional banks like America first, Chase, Golden west etc. These guys might have access to similar programs but maybe not near as many depending on the scope of their lending department. But oftentimes if you already bank with them they may have some

APPLY FOR A LOAN (PREQUALIFICATION)

lower rate or buydown incentives.
- **Rate:** Rate or interest rate is the percentage rate at which you are paying the bank/institution to borrow their money. The lower the rate the lower your monthly payment and subsequently, the less you pay them overtime.
- **30-year mortgage:** The standard length of time for a house payment. There are 15-year mortgages and a few others out there but for the most part you will be dealing with a 30-year mortgage.
- **Principal payment:** The amount of every monthly payment that is going to pay down the ACTUAL amount of your loan.
- **Interest payment:** The amount of each monthly payment that goes towards paying off the interest you owe to the bank. Note: The first few years of making payments will mostly be interest payments so do not be surprised if after a couple years you've paid $30,000 in mortgage payments but your loan amount has only gone down by $15,000. It sucks, I know, but as of right now and the last forever, this is how it is. But trust me, the pros far outweigh the cons!
- **Mortgage Insurance:** An amount of money added onto your monthly payment if you did not spend 20% or more for a down payment. The bank wants to know that they can make their money back if you default on the loan. So if you did not put 20% down then they are going to want a little extra every month until you've reached the equivalent of 20% down. Then it will drop off and your monthly payment will go down by however much the mortgage insurance was.
- **Refinance:** This is for after you have already taken a loan out and have a mortgage payment. If rates drop or you put down a large amount of money to pay off a chunk of the mortgage, you can refinance with your lender/bank to get the monthly payment lower. There are many reasons you may need a refi but this is the most common.

- **Conventional loan:** A type of loan that does not require governmental assistance. There are many programs within this loan type.
- **FHA Loan**: A government backed loan. These usually require the home to meet certain standards (it can't be a dump) in order for you to secure the loan. There are many programs within this loan type.
- **VA loan:** Loans provided exclusively to veterans of the military. There are some great programs here if you are a veteran. There are many programs within this loan type.
- **Rate buy down**: This is an option you have to spend money up front so that your interest rate is lower and therefore lowers you monthly payment. In other words, you can either spend it now or over the course of a 30-year mortgage.

One of the MOST COMMON questions I receive is, "Steve, when should I get prequalified? And wont it hurt my credit score?" Before I answer I want to mention, again, that I AM NOT a lender nor do I profess to be. Anything and everything I say about loans or the loan application process will be something you are going to want to go over with your preferred lender. Or if you don't have one, I am happy to point you in the direction of some fantastic ones.

I recommend reaching out to several and getting prequalified from MULTIPLE sources, bank and lender alike. Then you can see who has the better program that fits your specific needs or who you feel can help you the most.

The best time to get prequalified - in my opinion - is NOW. Even if you aren't going to buy a home for 6-8 months or a year or two. Getting prequalified is free. It may ding your credit score a couple of points, but nothing major (if I were you I wouldn't even be worrying about that side of things anyway unless you know you have terrible credit, in

APPLY FOR A LOAN (PREQUALIFICATION)

which case we have bigger problems and need to get you in touch with a credit repair specialist). By getting a stamp of approval from a bank or lender now gives you a leg up on EXACTLY where your financial capacities are and a birds-eye view as to what improvements you can make, if there are any needed.

Some realtors will argue with me on this and say that you should wait to get prequalified until you are 100% ready to buy a home, but to that I say, NUTS! In too many instances I have seen people wait until they find the home they love, try to buy it, but find out at the last minute that they can't due to financing reasons (that is to say - they can't get a loan). Maybe they had a problem with their credit but didn't know, or what if there was an old unpaid credit card from some obscure convenient store or perhaps they miscalculated their affordability index when they tried to run the numbers on their own.

In short, if you prepare and get prequalified sooner rather than later then you have a MUCH better shot at catching those errors upfront and fixing them before you find the house that works for you.

Perhaps one of those adjustments you'll need to make is a career change to a job that pays more for what your dreams and goals are. But you'll never know where you're at unless you get a professional's opinion. Most lenders will hold a prequalification for a few months, and you can always renew/update that as time goes on.

I've counseled with clients time and time again to not put themselves on the bench before even going to tryouts. Don't make the mistake of taking yourself out of the game before you've had a professional look at your situation and tell you where you stand and how to improve.

Not to mention, by getting prequalified you have expanded your team of people that are on your side and who want you to succeed! And now you have a lender/bank in your back pocket ready to help at a moment's notice. Your lender can help you navigate the complex inner workings of loaning money, interest rates, when to lock in, how much to put down to yield the highest return etc.

If you are working with a lender that charges you for the prequalification process, run the other way and come talk to me. I have several that will do it for free.

WHAT INFO WILL THE LENDER NEED FROM YOU

In order to get an accurate assessment, your lender/bank will need most of, if not all of, the following

- 2-3 years of past tax returns from all jobs
- Most recent 2-3 pay stubs
- Bank statements
- Retirement/401K account statements
- Personal identification such as name, birthday, drivers license
- Social security number.
- Maybe a few other things, but this will cover the bulk

Basically the lender is going to need to know exactly how much you make, how much you have saved and how much debt you have working against you. Once they gather all this information from you, they will plug it all into their software, move some things around and poof! You'll have a pretty good idea of how much you qualify for!

APPLY FOR A LOAN (PREQUALIFICATION)

DEBT TO INCOME RATIO

Your debt to income ratio is going to be the benchmark that will determine how much of a monthly payment you can afford and therefore how much home you can buy. Again, I am not a lender and you should verify all this information with a qualified professional but here's the gist. Most lenders want your DTI to be 50% or less. Meaning that they do not want your monthly mortgage payment to be more than 50% of your monthly income minus current debt.

Let's say you make $5,000 per month. That would put you right around $2,500 for a monthly payment. But now let's say that you have a car payment of $300 per month. Now we have to subtract that from the $2,500 to get $2,200. In this scenario you would be able to afford a $2,200 per month mortgage payment. Keep in mind that there is a LOT of leeway and many different scenarios and you definitely need to speak with a lender or bank so they can give you a customized quote.

Now that you've been prequalified you will be able to know exactly what price range to shop in. And when we find a home you particularly like we will be ready to submit an offer! FYI, The vast majority of home sellers WILL NOT even entertain an offer if it does not come with a preapproval letter from a lender or bank.

Just to reiterate so we're clear; I highly recommend shopping around to different lenders/banks. Even if you have a family member or friend who does it and can give you a good deal. You want someone who does it FULL TIME and comes with a great reputation. I'm sure you agree that when dealing with the LARGEST PURCHASE of your life, the last thing you want to do is entrust that to the neighbor friend who has only closed a handful of transactions in the last several years. Sure they might be able to close it out but at what cost and are you willing to risk it? In my experience, it's worth the extra few hundred dollars to hire a seasoned pro.

COSIGNING

Cosigning is when you add another person or persons to the loan in order to qualify for more money. Let's say that this is your first home and you are only qualifying for $295,000 on your own, which will not get you much of anything these days unfortunately. By having a co-singer jump onto the loan with you your qualifying power could increase to $350,000 or $400,000 which would put you in a much better position with more options.

Depending on how financially stable the cosigner is you could qualify for a whole lot more, but this is when you need to be cautious. You don't want to go buy a $500,000 home just because with a cosigner you can. Don't purchase more home than you are able to pay for with a monthly payment. Chances are your parents (or the cosigner, whoever it may be) agreed to help you, but that you still need to make all of the payments. That means that you will still need to keep the price in a range where you'll be able to afford the monthly payments.

Now you might be thinking, "Well Steve, if the bank/lender qualified me for a certain amount shouldn't I stay within the price range that they gave me?" The answer is yes and no. Depending on your specific situation you actually may be able to afford a higher monthly payment, but because of HOW you were qualified you might be in a much lower price range than you thought. Here are a few reasons why the

APPLY FOR A LOAN (PREQUALIFICATION)

qualification process might not be in your favor:

- You get paid in cash a lot at it is not necessarily all on tax records (non taxable income is generally not used as qualifying income)
- You are a business owner/entrepreneur and you know you can afford more but qualifying for more is proving very difficult. (Side note: being self employed and getting a loan is oftentimes difficult)
- You just got a new job but the lender/bank is qualifying you at your old/lower wages
- Your overtime hours or differential pay are not counted towards qualifying income even though they are mandated by your employer.
- You feel comfortable and and able to live a little more frugally than the bank/lender has given you as their parameters. Meaning that you are ok with a higher monthly mortgage payment than the bank/lender has given you as a cap. (Remember, the bank/lender WILL NOT qualify you for your maximum payment abilities, they air on the side of caution and want to make sure you have plenty of buffer)

There are MANY, MANY scenarios in which a cosigner is a very valid and fantastic option! Most of the time parents or close relatives are more than happy to help you get into your first home. Chances are, they are already planning on helping because they may have received help from their parents or family when they purchased their first home years ago. Give it some thought; cosigning may be the perfect fit for you if you are falling a little short on getting prequalified for a decent starter home.

3

Create a Must Have and a Nice to Have list

Now that you have been prequalified and know where you stand it's time to create your lists of what you want in a home. If you're like me then you probably started doing this before step one!

Before we dive into this chapter I want to be fully transparent with a crucial point. Sometimes if you are on the cusp of barely being able to afford a home then you are not going to be able to be very picky. It will still be a fantastic investment and spring you into your future, but you just might have to forgo the ¼ acre lot with a 3,000 sq ft home and a swimming pool in the backyard. In other words, be prepared to adjust your expectations based on how much a lender/bank will tell you that you qualify for.

You need to make TWO lists:

- **Must have:** These are things that you absolutely cannot do without; features in a home that are non-negotiable. Maybe it's that you have to have a house with at least 3 bedrooms because you have 2-3 kids.

CREATE A MUST HAVE AND A NICE TO HAVE LIST

Or maybe you need a 2 car garage because you run a part time auto shop and need a space for at least 1 car project and some tools. These are the absolute necessities.

- **Nice to have:** These are the features of a home that you would absolutely love but that are not 100% necessary. Perhaps you would really like 3 bathrooms but 2 would also be sufficient. Or maybe that fenced in backyard would be perfect but is not going to make it or break it.

The purpose of making these lists is to keep you grounded during the home search. It will help you narrow down what homes are more realistic for your specific situation. This list will be modified and changed as time goes on and as you see more homes. The best way to know what you want is to get out and take a look at the inventory!

MANAGING EXPECTATIONS

If you are a Billionaire then feel free to skip the rest of this chapter about managing expectations. For everyone else, please, continue.

The real estate market and/or your personal situation can change on the daily, and oftentimes does. You will need to be able to adapt and adjust with the times all while not losing sight of your goal (WHY). For example, let's say that today while we're looking for homes you currently qualify for $375,000 which can mostly get you everything you want. Let's say that tomorrow the interest rates go up or down, or maybe you have to spend a good chunk of money for a new car when yours breaks down. Life happens. Now, let's say you still qualify for $375,000 but home prices shot up $20,000 or perhaps you don't have as much for a downpayment as you would have liked.

That is ok. If you have successfully completed the challenge in chapter 1 then you already know that things will happen that may set you back. But you know what you're trying to do and can power through the obstacle easily!

> The principle is: The only things we know for certain are what's right in front of us. We can hope for better times or improved circumstances, but oftentimes we will have to adjust our expectations accordingly. Time and time again I've seen clients back out of a purchase for any number of reasons; however the majority of the time it is NOT due to legitimate or financial factors. Most of the time it is the 'cold feet' syndrome.

COLD FEET SYNDROME

We all know this very well. All of us at some time or another have chickened out from a dare, or eating a new food or trying a new thing etc. We find a mental objection and hold onto it for dear life. We convince ourselves that we cannot do that particular thing - whatever it may be - because of (insert your fear here).

Then a few moments later when the time to act has passed and you really start to think about it, you realize that you should have jumped, taken a bite, asked that girl out, or bought that house. Because now that the time for action has PASSED, you are able to put away those fears that stopped you initially and realize that you should have pulled the trigger. THIS IS WHY IT IS SO CRUCIAL TO FIND YOUR WHY AND WRITE IT DOWN. You can avoid missing your golden opportunity by

CREATE A MUST HAVE AND A NICE TO HAVE LIST

preparing before you even see a house.

My recommendation is that when you find a house that you feel good about and it checks 80% of your boxes or must have list, then you should seriously consider submitting an offer. Because who knows what will happen tomorrow; today we know you can buy that house. I'm definitely not saying to jump in blindfolded, but weigh the options, and if it logically makes sense and you feel it would ultimately be a good home for you, then push through the mental blockades and make it happen.

> Side note to keep in mind: This advice is primarily for first time home buyers or those who are NOT buying/building their forever or dream home. If it's your forever home and you have the money then by all means, make it happen!

4

Start Seeing Homes!

Now comes the fun part! We get to go see homes! Well almost, there is one more thing. The state of Utah, the NAR and all brokerage require the 'Buyer Broker' agreement to be signed BEFORE any homes are shown. This document is what EVERY buyer in the state of Utah must agree to before they purchase a home. We've been doing it in Utah for years so it's nothing new. In the past it's been a little bit of a gray area, but now, with new legislation, it will be mandated to be signed BEFORE seeing homes.

Key elements of this agreement bubble down to 3 things: Legal responsibility of the agent/brokerage to the client, protection and commissions.

1. **Legal representation/duties of the agent and client** - This agreement specifies exactly what the Realtor is going to do for you, how he/she is to act and that EVERYTHING is to be done with the utmost level of integrity and honesty.
2. **Protection** - We as real estate professionals are LEGALLY bound by the Code of Ethics. We literally HAVE to maintain a high level

of business dealings. This only protects you more. It also protects the real estate agent from shady clients who try to glean everything they can from the realtor and then dump them in the dirt as soon as all the pieces fall into place. Believe it or not, this has happened to me and there are some very sleazy people out there just waiting to take advantage of good, hard working and honest individuals.

3. **Commissions** - This document delineates the commissions owed to the brokerage from the buyer in the event that the client purchases a home. This is usually 2.5%-3% but can be negotiated. <u>The vast majority of the time the selling party will pay for that out of their proceeds so you as a buyer do not have to come up with that cash out of pocket.</u> However, with full transparency, a seller can refuse to pay for the buyer's agent commission. I have never had this happen, but it is a possibility. You as the buyer may still be responsible for paying for that commission to your Realtor if you buy the house. But rest assured if your Realtor is any good he/she should be able to find a creative way to make that work.

Most Agents have spent countless hours and years researching, studying, working to become the best in their industry and on the cutting edge of the most relevant real estate happenings. The market changes EVERY DAY! The principle of hiring quality vs cheap is maintained across all service oriented professions. If you want something done right with a warranty and peace of mind then it is going to cost more than a discounted service would. I highly recommend you look up the Ship Repair Man Story online and give it a quick read! It'll only take you a couple min.

Ok! So now we start seeing homes!! Your Realtor will start sending you homes based off of the criteria you created in the previous chapter. Feel free to do your own searches as well, sometimes multiple eyes looking around yield more results. When you find one that is of some interest you'll want to let your realtor know and he/she will contact the sellers and coordinate a showing time and date.

When you enter any home for a showing please treat it as if it were a billion dollar mansion. Or in other words, be gentle, don't break anything and take off your shoes if asked. Feel free to open doors, drawers, cabinets, turn on and off lights, water faucets etc. Basic functions of the home need to be tested. If something is stuck or not working right please stop what you're doing and get your Realtor. The last thing we'd want is for something to break or get jammed. If it doesn't move, turn on or do what it's supposed to with relative ease then it may be broken and we will want to contact the sellers before we do anything else with that particular item or area of the house.

Take special note of the main features of the house such as:

- Roof
- Water Heater
- Air Conditioner
- Furnace
- Windows
- Electrical box
- Plumbing (If accessible)
- Any visible water damage or significant concrete shifting

Anything that looks old, broken or in need of repair can be highlighted to a home inspector later on.

5

Writing The Offer

Once we find a home that is up to snuff and has most of what you want, then we need to submit an offer. Even if the offer is a little low it can't hurt, the worst thing a seller can do is say no. I'm not going to go into great detail with everything that is included in an offer but will give you the highlights. It's a long document and you are more than welcome to read it or I can go over it with you in detail.

It is called the Real Estate Purchase Contract or REPC. For the purpose of keeping things simple I will explain the following elements of an offer: purchase price, earnest money, down payment, closing costs, new Loan amount, subject to sale, home warranty, seller disclosures, due diligence, appraisal condition, settlement, addendums.

- **Purchase price**: pretty self explanatory. This is the TOTAL amount that you are offering for the property.
- **Earnest money**: This is a good faith payment. It is due 4 days after we go under contract, meaning once the sellers accept the offer. This money is deposited into the brokerage account and goes

toward the purchase of the home. THIS IS NOT EXTRA MONEY on top of the purchase price. If you back out of the purchase before the due diligence deadline then you can get that money back (more on this date later). If you back out after that deadline then the money goes to the seller as compensation.

- **Down payment:** The total amount of cash you are going to use to pay down your loan amount. (Side note: there are loan programs out there for 0% down, 1% down, 3% down 5% down, 20% down or really any amount)
- **Closing costs:** NOT part of the down payment. This money DOES NOT go toward paying down your loan. This is the cost to purchase the home. It can include fees such as, loan origination, title fees, insurance fees, brokerage fees, county recording fees etc. Simply put, this is cash you will need to bring to the closing table that will be directly withdrawn from your bank account. I usually tell my clients to plan on between 2%-3% of the purchase price, but can vary quite a bit depending on the situation. Sometimes it's less, sometimes it's a little more.
- **New loan amount:** This is the number that will be used to start your 30 year mortgage. So if your purchase price of a home was $400,000 and you put $15,000 down, then your new loan amount would be $385,000
- **Subject to sale:** This is when you need to sell a home before purchasing the next one. If you are a first-time homebuyer then you will not fall into this category, but I thought I'd mention it. If this is you, then there is additional paperwork and contingencies that we will need to discuss.
- **Home warranty**: There is a section on the REPC where we can elect to include a home warranty in the sale of the home.
- **Seller disclosure deadline**: This is the date when the sellers need to give us ALL the information they know about the house, any

WRITING THE OFFER

repairs they had, and damages, upgrades, floods, fires etc. It's due usually a couple days after going under contract.

- **Due diligence deadline**: This is a period of time in which you will want to do a home inspection by a licensed home inspector. You're not going to be doing this until you go under contract on the home. It is not required but I highly recommend it so you know what you're buying. If there are issues large enough that you want to have fixed then we will reopen negotiations with the sellers to see what we can work out. A home inspection costs around $400-$600 depending on what you have inspected and what home inspection company you use.
- **Financing and appraisal deadline**: This is the date by which you as the buyer need to have all your financing figured out. This means that your loan officer will want to have everything regarding your loan done and ready to rock and roll. (Side note: sometimes the underwriting process can take longer and they may need you to submit additional/updated information as time goes on. If this happens we can renegotiate some of the dates with the sellers.)
- **Settlement deadline**: This is the latest date by which both parties will need to have signed the final paperwork. Settlement can occur before this deadline, but not after (unless we write up an addendum stating the changes).
- **Addendum**: These are additional pieces of paper included with an offer that have extra terms not included in the REPC. Examples can be if you are using an FHA loan, if you want to ask for closing costs to be paid by the seller, if you are related to one or more of the Agents involved. Basically it's a way to include anything else in the offer that we need to.

Once we have gone over each element of the offer and you feel comfortable with what's being presented you will then need to sign the document(s). Most of the time that will be via docusign or a similar online program. But if you're old school and want to see the physical piece of paper in person I can definitely make that happen.

There are response deadlines included on the REPC so the sellers can't take forever to respond. Usually we will have a response within 1-2 business days. That response can come in 1 of 3 different forms.

1. **Acceptance**: the sellers flat out accept all our terms and conditions and we are under contract!
2. **Counter offer**: The sellers accept most of our terms but reply with a modification of some sort.
3. **Rejection:** They rejected our offer.

Obviously the best case scenario is when the sellers accept your offer and we are off to the races! But that rarely happens. Most of the time people want to negotiate and see if they can get anything more than is currently on the table. If the seller's counter back then the roles have reversed and you are now in the driver's seat to either accept, counter or reject their counter-offer.

This goes on until both sides reach a consensus or one or the other kills the deal. Some of this negotiation may occur verbally but NOTHING is binding unless it is in writing AND signed by both parties. This is where it pays to have hired a professional who knows what he/she is doing; and your chances of getting what you want without problems increase tenfold.

If I were to go into each possible scenario related to negotiation tactics, strategies and possible outcomes you would never finish this book! There are endless ways to negotiate and craft offer/counter offers.

WRITING THE OFFER

Having someone on your team who is a full time realtor and has seen countless scenarios is INVALUABLE when you need to get creative during the negotiation process.

6

Under Contract

Congrats!! You're under contract!! Which means you beat out other potential buyers and now have the exclusive opportunity to buy the home as long as everything checks out. You've heard the term 'Under Contract' in this book and probably a few times before just talking to people about buying homes. All this means is that you have two parties that have both agreed to the terms to sell a house, it is in writing and both sides have SIGNED the document. A typical time period from start to finish is about 1-2 months. Meaning, once you go under contract the home will be yours within 1-2 months. A lot has to happen in that time frame as discussed below.

SELLER PROPERTY CONDITION DISCLOSURES

Within a few days of going under contract the sellers will deliver to us a large document that will specify any and everything that they know about the house. This can be anything from undergrads and renovations, to damages or small little quirks. It is in the seller's best interest to disclose everything they know no matter how small. This is given to us for review and will need to be signed and sent back acknowledging that you have received and seen the disclosures.

If applicable, they will also give to us any and all HOA related documents and amendments as well as any CCR's (covenants, conditions and restrictions for the neighborhood.)

DUE DILIGENCE

Once you are under contract you enter your due diligence time period and need to turn in your earnest money. You will have 4 days to make out a check or wire the money to the brokerage or title company (whoever has been designated to hold those funds in escrow). Remember, this can be given back to you if you cancel the deal before your due diligence period is over. There are some instances in which you can get that money back after your due diligence period. If that happens then we can cross that bridge when we get there. For all intensive purposes, I highly recommend using the due diligence deadline as your hard cut off for when your earnest money becomes non refundable.

The due diligence time period is typically around 10-14 days but can vary depending on what was negotiated before going under contract. This is when you have the chance to hire a home inspector, contractor, electrician, plumber, roofer, HVAC guy or whoever you want to inspect the home. A general home inspection will cost between $400-$600. And if you have a specialist like a roofer or an electrician then you will have to get their rates for inspections.

If, for some reason, something is largely wrong with an element of the home then, you as the buyer, have another opportunity to negotiate repairs to be made on the home. You can pursue one of the following 3 options

1. Try and have the seller's fix the issue(s) before the sale is finalized
2. Pursue some sort of monetary compensation ie., lower the purchase price, ask for seller paid closing costs or seller paid rate buy down for your loan etc.
3. A hybrid of the two examples above

In the event the sellers refuse to help with repairs (if there are any to be made) then you as the buyer, have the option to either kill the deal and get your earnest money back or continue on with the purchase.

When purchasing a home with an FHA loan, there may be required repairs. FHA backed loans have to ensure the home meets certain safety standards. If, for whatever reason, the FHA appraiser deems there to be required repairs, then those HAVE to be completed before you would be able to get a loan for the house. The same negotiating rules apply; if you can have the sellers help make all the fixes, great! If not then you will have to decide if you want to make the repairs/pay for a contractor to fix the items (with the seller's consent) before purchasing the home.

If you are purchasing the home with a Conventional loan or in Cash then the required repairs situation does not apply. In other words, even if there are repairs to be made, you can still get a loan or purchase the property without having to have those repairs remedied before buying the home.

There are many other strange scenarios that can, and have occurred, but these scenarios and examples are the most common. If you do happen to venture out into the unknown with an odd situation then your Realtor should be able to help navigate possible options and outcomes.

FINANCING AND APPRAISAL

Once the home is under contract the lender and title company will get to work. The lender will start to push your loan through the system, they may ask for more info or updated information such as most recent pay stubs or new bank statements etc.

The lender will also order an appraisal. This means that a licensed appraiser will go to the property to determine if the under contract value - purchase price - is valid. The appraisers job is NOT TO DETERMINE THE VALUE OF THE HOME, but to validate that the agreed upon sales price is credible. Basically the lender/bank needs to know that they can get their money back should you, the borrower, default on the loan and then they -the bank/lender - had to turn around and sell the property.

The Title company will also begin a comprehensive background search of the property to ensure that there is nothing fishy going on. They want to make sure that there are not any liens on the property. And that there are not any current lawsuits involving the property or that the current owners on title are in fact the legitimate owners. There are many background checks they perform to ensure that the purchase is a clean transaction.

That is all stuff that's going on behind the scenes. Once you have finished with the due diligence items or repairs, if any, then there is not much else for you, as the buyer, to do. For the last two weeks or so of the under contract period we are essentially waiting for all the other parties involved to get their ducks in a row. So do not be worried if you do not hear from anyone for a few days. We will most definitely keep you updated, but sometimes we just have to hurry up and wait.

Two things you can do as you near the closing/settlement deadline is 1. call all of the utility companies and start to switch them over to your name and 2. Start finding a homeowners insurance company you like (your lender will require you to have homeowners insurance).

UTILITIES AND HOMEOWNERS INSURANCE

About a week before closing you should start calling the utility companies to get the ball rolling (Sewer, Water, Gas, Power etc). Depending on the city/county you can sometimes have them set up to start in your name on a certain future date. Other times the utility company wont allow the change to be made until you have proof you now own the home. If this is the case then the title company will tell you which document is best to use for that verification.

If you have not done so already then now would be a good time to shop around for different homeowners insurance companies. Homeowners insurance is something that no homeowner should be without. The LAST thing you want is to not be insured and then have the house burn down. Then you're stuck making loan payments for a pile of rubble with no way to recoup the loss. The majority of the time it will be required by your lender anyway. All homeowners insurance agencies will have similar plans but their pricing may differ. Find someone you trust to get you started.

> Side note: It seems like homeowners insurance companies will start to increase the premium payments you make after about 3-5 years. They may get you a decent deal upfront, but after a few years it would be wise to keep an eye on the payments/statements and see if they increase. It's never a bad idea to price shop when the topic comes up. It also helps if you bundle auto and home insurance together. For me personally, it seems like we switch our insurance company every 3-4 years.

7

The Closing and Post Settlement

Once the title company has finished its background checks and the lender gives us the 'clear to close,' then you'll receive a couple documents to review. The title company will send you a settlement statement and the lender/bank will send you closing disclosures. You'll want to look these over and make sure that it's exactly what you were expecting. If you have questions on those then you'll want to reach out to either the lender or title company.

The settlement statement is a birds eye view of the transaction and how all the numbers are going to be either credited or debited; it's usually only a page or two and is pretty straight forward.

The closing disclosures are a bit more lengthy and go into more detail than the settlement statement. If I were you I'd hop on the phone and have your lender walk you through those disclosures just so there is 100% transparency and you know EXACTLY what's going on. There is nothing worse than getting to the closing table and looking down at the documents and having the numbers/stipulations NOT be what you thought.

THE CLOSING AND POST SETTLEMENT

If everything looks good then we set a time, date and location to meet up to sign a big stack of papers! The title company will facilitate the closing. You will need to bring two forms of ID (although you may only be asked for one). Title will prepare all of the documents, explain what each means and collect the funds via wire transfer - or cashiers check if it's under $10,000.

WIRE FRAUD

Beware of all the scams out there. DO NOT send any money anywhere unless you receive the instructions in person from the title company. Scammers are getting very creative and will send emails and letters or even call you on the phone and impersonate the title company, lender or Realtor and tell you to send the down payment somewhere. DO NOT send it without first checking with a couple trusted sources. If you do send that money you will never get it back.

FUNDING AND RECORDING

Once you have signed all of the papers you are what I like to call a 99.9% homeowner. The only thing left to do BEFORE you can get keys to the home is for the title company to fund and record the sale. This means that all the funds must be properly distributed to each respective entity that was involved. AND the county must get paid and record the sale on the county records.

This funding and recording process will usually happen on the same day of the close IF all the documents were signed BEFORE 11 am or so. If you or the seller signed the closing documents after about 12 pm then changes are the sale will not fund and record until the next morning.

I always recommend planning on not receiving the keys for 24-48 hours after signing just to be on the safe side. Although most of the time it happens pretty quickly!

POST SETTLEMENT

CONGRATS!! You bought a house!! Now that it's yours there are several things you'll want to do and be aware of. Here's a list of to-do's:

- Re key all of the locks and change any electronic codes (including garage door.) I always recommend this being one of the first things you do. That way the long lost drunk cousin of the previous owners that shows up late at night and tries to let himself into the house to pass out on the floor can't get in...
- Get all of the utilities changed over into your name to avoid them being shut off. You should have started this process before closing, so if it's not done yet you'll need to do that ASAP. Or you may find yourself without water, power or heat.
- Homeowners insurance. Same as the utilities. If you haven't done this yet then you need to do it ASAP. The last thing you want is for the house to burn down or a tree to fall on the roof without being covered by homeowners insurance. And besides, your lender will most likely require it anyway.
- Make sure you know where the water shut off and gas shut off valves to the house are and how to operate them.
- Keep an eye out for any quirks or strange things about the house that we can ask the previous homeowners about. Most people are usually willing to help answer questions for a few weeks or even a

THE CLOSING AND POST SETTLEMENT

month after they have moved out. But the longer you wait to ask questions the more annoyed they may get and just ignore us.
- You will receive lots of junk mail, emails or phone calls for the first several months. Stuff like "Your home warranty is going to expire" or "This is your second notice, please pay your bill to the company," or "Your title company didn't receive the documents, send us everything you have." Lots of the time it will look legitimate, if that is the case then send a picture to your realtor and they will be able to tell you if it's real or a scam. But in any case, don't send anything to anyone unless you have double checked.
- Post office/mail. If you now live in a community/subdivision/town home and your mailbox is a post office box then you'll need to get with the HOA to get new keys. Or even sometimes you will have to go directly to the post office to get things rolling with your new mailing address. You may need to re key the mail box depending on how the post office handles that particular community. And be sure to update any mail subscriptions to go to your new home or set up forwarding addresses with the post office.
- Over the course of the next year you will learn all about basic homeowner responsibilities such as yard maintenance (if you have a yard), changing your furnace filter regularly, cleaning gutters during the fall so they don't clog up and flood your basement, cover your A/C unit before winter, spray for bugs every month or two, the best way to shovel your driveway, and lots of new little things.

Please don't hesitate to ever reach out to your Realtor. If they are a professional and good at their job then they will have all sorts of contacts for plumbers, electricians, carpet cleaners, house cleaners, window washers, handymen, sewer pump guys etc. Whatever comes up, your Realtor will have someone that can fix it or point you in the right direction.

Sometime within the week following your purchase the seller's Realtor should come by to pick up their sign and lock box. Please don't move or do anything with the sign or lock box unless you receive instruction to do so. If the seller's agent does not come by within the first week then you can have your Realtor reach out to them to get it taken care of.

8

Summary

See, that wasn't so bad! Now you are ready to get after it and can create a road map for your future by following these basic steps:

1. Understand WHY you are buying the home (investment, lifestyle, stepping stone, legacy etc...)
2. Write your reasons down, make a small vision board somewhere that you can see it EVERY DAY.
3. Talk to several lenders and/or banks to get prequalified.
4. Make your 'Must have' and 'Nice to have' lists.
5. Contact your Realtor and tell them you want to start seeing homes.
6. Find the right home that fits most of what is on your 'Must have' list.
7. Put an offer together.
8. Negotiate.
9. Go under contract on the home.
10. Order a home inspection.
11. Negotiate again if repairs need to be made.
12. Work with your lender/bank and title company throughout

the process. Maybe start getting utilities and homeowners insurance set up a few days before settlement
13. Meet up with the Title company and sign that stack of papers everyone always talks about.
14. When the home funds and records, THEN you are the homeowner, not before.
15. Get keys!!
16. Make sure all the utilities are in your name.
17. Finalize your homeowners insurance company and policy.
18. CELEBRATE and have a house warming BBQ party! I'll bring the drinks and a dessert!

YOU DID IT!!! Now you can consider yourself looped into the basics of buying a home. If you liked this book and found it helpful, please head on over to amazon, type in the title and leave me a 5 star review! I would be incredibly grateful. Or you could even go to my Google page 'Stephen Dredge Real Estate' and leave a 5 star review there! And as always any suggestions or recommendations are always appreciated! This book is intended to be a work in progress and added onto to stay updated with the times.

9

Bonus Chapter: ROI and Investment Basics

Return on Investment or ROI - When you start renting

Let's dive into how you calculate ROI. This is when you compare the final value of an investment with what it cost you to start that investment to give you a percentage. That percentage tells you how much you made (or lost) on any particular investment. Time to do some math. See the return on investment formula below.

Financial ROI Formula
$$\frac{\text{Return on}}{\text{Investment}} = \frac{\text{Net Profit}}{\text{Cost of Investment}} \times 100$$

Project ROI Formula
$$\frac{\text{Return on}}{\text{Investment}} = \frac{\text{Financial Value} - \text{Project Cost}}{\text{Project Cost}} \times 100$$

ROI = Your returned amount divided by your initial investment multiplied by 100 to get a percentage. Another way of saying it is: what you make is divided by what you spent multiplied by 100.

This will give you a percentage. For example: if you purchased $400 of Apple stock and then later sold that stock for $500, then your ROI would be ((500-400)/400)X100 = .25. Or, in other words your return on that investment is 25%.

In the stock market, casinos, horse races, and virtually everywhere, there exists only one dimensional returns on those "investments". In real estate, however, there are FOUR different ways in which you can receive a return on your investment. And they ADD onto each other. You don't have to pick and choose which one to use. You get to use them all.

4 TYPES OF RETURNS IN REAL ESTATE

1. Cash flow - This is if you rent the house out for more than the mortgage payment
2. Principal reduction - This is having someone else pay for your principal and interest payments
3. Appreciation - This is the natural rate of appreciation that happens to your house.
4. Cost segregation and/or Taxes (I won't go into this one as you will want to reach out to your CPA for further guidance on this topic.

Let's go through a basic example using the following criteria/numbers. You can plug the following numbers into a mortgage calculator online to give you the principal payment amount. And remember that we are looking for a YEARLY return. So all of our answers will need to

BONUS CHAPTER: ROI AND INVESTMENT BASICS

be converted to have the same common denominator of 1 year or 12 months (not 1 month)

- Purchase price of the home = $500,000
- Down Payment = $50,000
- New Loan amount = $400,000
- 30 Year mortgage @ 7% interest rate
- Annual appreciation rate = 4% (this is a conservative average appreciation rate)
- Monthly payment = $3,523
- Rental amount from tenants per month = $3,600
- First years average Principal payment per month = $385 (I got this by plugging the information into a mortgage calculator and looking at the 30 year amortization schedule. As the years progress the amount the principal payment will increase and the interest amounts will decrease)

Cash flow

To calculate cash flow you simply subtract the monthly payment from the rental amount like this: $3,600 - $3,523 = $77. Now you Divide the $77 increase by your initial investment and multiply by 100 like this: (77/50,000)X100 = .15%. This tells you that your MONTHLY return for the cash flow is .15%. For the year total it would be 1.85% return.

Principal reduction

To calculate principal reduction we take the average first year's principal payment of $385 and multiply it by 12 (so it's the yearly return and not monthly return) to get $4,620. Now we divide that by the initial investment and multiply by 100 like this: (4,620/50,000)X100 = 9.24% return!

Appreciation

To calculate the annual appreciation we multiply the total house price by the appreciation rate like this: $500,000X.04 = $20,000. Now we divide the appreciated dollar amount by the initial investment and multiply by 100 like this: (20,000/50,000)X100 = 40% return!

TOTAL

Now for the fun part. We add up the total 3 types of returns to get the FIRST years return on our investment like this 1.85% + 9.24% + 40% = **51.09%!!!** In other words, because you spent $50,000 to buy the home you are getting back 51.09% of that $50,000 in the first year! This translates into the forms of somebody else paying down the loan, somebody else paying for you to have a home appreciate, and someone else paying you rent on which your making a little bit of money.

A FEW THINGS TO THINK ABOUT

- IT GETS EVEN BETTER! This is only for the FIRST year. For the second year your cash flow will increase if you raise rents and therefore increase your cash flow % return, your principal reduction amounts will increase to around $400 per month or $4,800 per year which increases your principal reduction amount % return, and appreciation will continue doing its thing! EVERY year your ROI

BONUS CHAPTER: ROI AND INVESTMENT BASICS

will increase and keep increasing!
- Don't get ahead of yourself. You need to buy your first home before any of this can happen. And chances are you'll be living in that home so none of this applies. But after a few years, if you've prepared and saved, you'll be able to purchase your second home and start renting the first one out at which point you can start implementing this formula!
- You might be saying "Well Steve you're wrong right now you can't cash flow on a property unless you put a massive amount of money down up front!" (rents are lower than the mortgage payment). You are 100% correct. If your cash flow is negative then that would be working against your total ROI. Let's imagine, using the example above, that you could only rent that home for $2800 per month. When we do the math we find that the return on the cash flow side of things is NEGATIVE 17.35%.

Now if we add that to our other two returns on investment we still come out with a whopping 31.89%!! You would still have to supplement $725 per month to make the mortgage payment. But look at it this way, you are investing $725 per month to make over 31% return. And after the first year you'd want to add $8,700 to your $50,000 initial investment to increase the number you divide everything out by $58,700.

> There are a few more moving parts if you don't positive cash flow right out of the gate; but over time your rents will increase, principal amount will be reduced and you might even be able to refinance at a lower rate at some point. Within a few years you will start to break even on cash flows and not have to supplement any of the monthly payment!

To put this all into perspective, think about other forms of investing ie,.

Roth IRA, retirement funds, mutual funds, etc that yield a 4% to maybe 10% return depending on how aggressive the portfolios are. It makes you start to wonder. Food for thought :)

Testimonials

TESTIMONIALS

"Stephen has been incredible during this house buying experience! He has a great attitude, has stood up for us, and was able to provide a great assortment of houses while adventuring around with us. He truly wanted us to be happy with the decision we were making and helped my fiance and I collect OUR thoughts about what WE wanted. Not only was the house buying experience great, but he has continually made aware to us all the scams that are out there that come with buying a house. If you want a Realtor that truly has your hack and isn't just out there to make a sale. Stephen is your guy! We have since moved into our house and seen many of those scams tactics that he warned us about. We insider Stephen to be a dear friend of ours."
  -Kyle

"I've never sold a home before, let alone one which had been in our family for over 60 years. I didn't know the first thing about it when I was introduced to Stephen Dredge. Stephen explained, in plain English, and made me feel comfortable with the process. The home needed some TLC to be ready to sell, Stephen has access to a network of professionals to handle the services we required.

He kept me informed in a timely manner, and communicated my concerns to the buyers and their agent. I would definitely recommend Stephen Dredge and his Real Estate Agency for those in need of his services."

- Brad

"Steve is a champion! He helped me transition through the selling and purchasing process. Steve is very knowledgeable with the processes, and is dependable and trustworthy. Steve put in the extra efforts to make the situation successful! I highly recommend Steve!"

-Brian

"My wife and I had to sell our home very quickly in order for us to move across the country. Stephen was amazing and helped us sell the home and make some money. He made the process smooth and easy for us. If I could give 6 stars I would!"

-Braden

"Stephen has sold a few homes for me and he's always been very proactive and does everything he can to make sure our sales go as smoothly as possible. He cares about his customers. I would Highly recommend Stephen."

-Ryan

"My wife I needed to sell a home in Ogden Utah, we listed it ourselves and no such luck. Stephen Dredge got ahold of us among a few other real estate people and we really liked Stephen from the get go. He was very kind and respectful so we decided to use him to list our house and we couldn't be happier this guy went above and beyond any expectations you would expect from a real estate person. You will not be disappointed if you go with Stephen!"

TESTIMONIALS

-Justin

"We had such a great experience selling our house with Stephen. He always responded in a timely manner to all our questions. We knew we could trust his local knowledge and felt his support throughout the process. Highly recommend using Stephen as your Utah realtor."

-Rachel

"I've know Stephen since college, and even though I have other friends in the real estate business, he's the one I wanted to help me navigate a home sale and subsequent home purchase. Just a solid dude all around and I knew he would ultimately have my best interest in mind and would work hard to make it happen. This was particularly important as I wasn't able to be in the area myself for the majority of the process. Communication was always top notch, even when I was in very different time zones. What I didn't know coming into the experience was the depth of knowledge that he had on the specific area that I was looking to buy in. He really hooked us up with a dream build in an area we were really excited about. He definitely went above and beyond in keeping us informed, stopping by our new house to take pictures of the progress, and communicating our vision with the builder. Great experience overall."

-Braiden

"Stephen made our first time home buying experience a breeze! He answered every question we had and was there for us day and night! (Literally) He's so nice and has your back throughout the entire process. The best realtor out there!"

-Madi

"Couldn't recommend Steve more! He helped my fiancé and I purchase our first home, and he was patient, knowledgable, and quick to respond throughout the whole process. Great communication, understands the local market, and a great guy too!"
-Amanda

"Stephen really pulled it off for us on our house, we were on our last string... he helped us in every situation we had. We highly recommend Stephen and would use him again if needed."
-Jordan

"I recently had the pleasure of working with Stephen for the second time; he has helped me navigate both the buying and selling process of my home. From our first interaction a few years ago to this most recent sale, Stephen has been nothing short of incredible.

Stephen's friendliness makes every step of the real estate process enjoyable. His approachable demeanor and genuine care for his clients' needs create a comfortable and trusting environment. It's rare to find someone who treats your real estate transactions with as much care and respect as if they were his own.

What truly sets Stephen apart, though, is his in-depth knowledge of the real estate market. His insights and advice are always spot-on, demonstrating a deep understanding of the nuances that can make or break a deal. This expertise has been invaluable to me, providing clarity and confidence in making informed decisions.

Additionally, Stephen's helpfulness cannot be overstated. Whether it's offering advice on staging a home for sale, navigating the complexities of paperwork, or simply being available to answer questions at a moment's notice, Stephen consistently goes above and beyond. His dedication to his clients is evident in every interaction, and it's this level of service that truly makes him stand out.

For anyone looking to buy or sell a home, I cannot recommend Stephen highly enough. His combination of friendliness, real estate knowledge, and unwavering commitment to his clients make him an exceptional choice. Thank you, Stephen, for making what could have been a stressful process both successful and enjoyable."

-Trevor

"Steve is a great realtor and an even better person. We really connected with him throughout our house shopping journey and he made us feel very comfortable with the process as a whole. His work was prompt and accurate with solid local knowledge and he would respond to me in a timely manner when needed. His background in the area helped us establish trust for his work. He's a great guy. Would work with him again!"

-Kenny

See my Google reviews and Zillow review pages online for more testimonials.

About the Author

- Currently active licensed Realtor in the state of Utah since November 2020
  - Full time Realtor since August 2022.
  - Currently partnered with Cade Erickson at ReMax Associates (Layton).
  - License #9311115-SA00

EDUCATION

Utah State University
Graduation: Fall 2019 – Bachelors; International Business — Minor; Portuguese
My clients love that I have a 4-year college degree in business that I can draw on daily to help them negotiate and buy/sell their home.
Very few Realtors have a 4 year degree, most fell into the industry on a whim. This is what I Intentionally chose after completing a formal education.

Study Abroad – Internships

Ghana Africa; 3 months – teaching business classes to local entrepreneurs. Assisted our partner sponsor - Mentors International - with their business.

Paris France; 2 weeks – Meeting with International companies like Coca Cola and Windows, touring their facilities and learning from the best and brightest.

PRIOR TO FULL TIME REAL ESTATE WORK EXPERIENCE

United States Cold Storage – Assistant Superintendent
Fall 2021-Fall 2022

-I was brought on to help reform and recreate a program that was failing. During my time here, I managed a 24/7-hour team with 6 different shifts, assisted in the hiring and firing processes, communicated with ALL suppliers for daily needed materials and safety equipment amongst many other things. In essence, I recreated and ran half of the warehouse CIW program which employed 40-50 people all while overseeing millions of dollars' worth of product each day. By the time I left, the program that had been on the brink of being shut down was upright, humming and making more money than any other program in the company.

Coldsweep Dry Ice Blasting Solutions – Superintendent
2012-2020

- My clients love the fact that I am not afraid of hard work. At Coldsweep I oversaw and worked on projects that were extremely physically demanding in some of the most unique places in the country. When nobody else could get the job done that's when they called us. Anything from fine tuning the paint job of vintage sports cars to working on and cleaning hydroelectric generators underneath a lake 3/4 of a mile underground so that entire cities could have power.

SS Johnson Construction – Field Technician
2017-2019

People that hire me love that I can draw on a construction background when they are looking for homes to buy, build or sell. At my time building steel buildings I was able to assist in building structures that ranged from Barndominiums in the back yard to massive warehouses bigger than 3 football fields long.

Other things to note:

- I am a homeowner myself and actively investing in the market
    - I am a top 250 Realtor for the NWAR in 2023
    - Eagle Scout; Boy Scouts of America
    - Fluent in Portuguese (basic Spanish)
    - 2-year non-profit service in Angola Africa
    - I have 2 beautiful daughters and an amazingly gorgeous wife!

Here are just a few of the many reasons why my clients choose to work with me:

- I have been in Real estate for several years (and yes, during the covid-19 pandemic).
    - I AM FULL TIME.
    - I partner with Cade Erickson who has been in the business for 20+ years. We have a team of 5 people who meet together twice a week to discuss the market, the homes we have for sale, our clients,

demographics, statistics, best practices etc. This ensures we are on the cutting edge of everything Real Estate related, keeping your best interests in mind. Nobody else has meetings and trainings like we do.

- I also have a full-time assistant to ensure you have the smoothest experience possible.

- If we are selling your home, I will order and pay for a professional photo package – The first impression people have these days is online so the home needs to look good.

- Professional drone video footage and online advertising

- I have trusted relationships with all sorts of contractors (plumbers, roofers, HVAC technicians, landscapers, inspectors, handymen, title company, lenders, electricians etc). If questions arise, I can point you in the right direction.

- Most Agents sell 2.8 homes per year and therefore are not up to date with the current market (it's constantly changing). I sell 12-24 homes per year which gives me much more experience from every aspect of real estate.

-I have trusted relationships with several builders and am very familiar with the new construction process.

www.ingramcontent.com/pod-product-compliance
Lightning Source LLC
Chambersburg PA
CBHW070127230526
45472CB00004B/1453